The

HOLY SPIRIT

and

REALITY

WATCHMAN NEE

Living Stream Ministry
Anaheim, California • www.lsm.org

First Edition, August 2001.

ISBN 0-7363-0628-5

Published by

Living Stream Ministry
2431 W. La Palma Ave., Anaheim, CA 92801 U.S.A.
P. O. Box 2121, Anaheim, CA 92814 U.S.A.

Printed in the United States of America

06 07 / 9 8 7 6 5 4 3 2

CONTENTS

PREFACE

The message in this book touches a great matter in the Christian life—the Holy Spirit and reality. With concrete examples, it demonstrates that behind everything spiritual there is the reality. This reality is in the Holy Spirit, and the Holy Spirit leads men into the knowledge of this reality. The appendix after the message deals with one type of Christian sickness: obsession. It points out the phenomenon and causes of obsession as well as the way to divine deliverance.

THE HOLY SPIRIT AND REALITY

Scripture Reading: John 4:24; 16:13; 1 John 5:6

God's children must realize that in God's eyes, every spiritual thing and matter has its reality. If we merely touch the outward appearance without touching the reality, what we touch has no spiritual value. What is the reality of a spiritual thing? The reality of a spiritual thing is spiritual; it is not physical. Although spiritual realities must be expressed in words, words alone are often not the reality. Although spiritual reality is expressed in our daily lives, legalistic formalities are not realities. Although spiritual reality is manifested through our behavior, human performance is not reality.

WHAT IS SPIRITUAL REALITY?

What then is spiritual reality? The Lord said that "God is Spirit, and those who worship Him must worship in spirit and truthfulness" (John 4:24). The word "truthfulness" can be translated as "reality." The Lord also said, "But when He, the Spirit of reality, comes, He will guide you into all the reality" (16:13). First John 5:6 says, "The Spirit is He who testifies, because the Spirit is the reality." This shows us that God is Spirit, and everything related to God has to be in spirit. The Spirit of truth is the Spirit of reality. Hence, spiritual reality must be in the Holy Spirit. Spiritual reality is something that transcends people and things. Only that which is in the Holy Spirit is spiritual reality. All spiritual things are sustained in the Holy Spirit. Once a spiritual thing moves away from the Holy Spirit, it becomes letter and form, and it is dead. All spiritual things must be in the Holy Spirit before they can be real, living, and organic. The Holy Spirit leads us into all reality. Hence, any experience that we can acquire without the guidance of the Holy Spirit is surely not spiritual reality. Anything that we acquire through our ears, our mind, or our emotion alone is not spiritual reality. Only the things that the Holy Spirit guides us into are spiritual reality. We have to remember that the Holy Spirit is the Executor of all spiritual things. Whatever God is doing today is executed by the Holy Spirit. Only that which the Holy Spirit does is real, and only that is reality.

Everything that is in the Holy Spirit is reality. When man touches reality, he touches life. Life and reality are joined together. If a man wants to take care of the spiritual life, he has to take care of spiritual reality. If a man touches spiritual reality in the Holy Spirit, he will immediately respond when others touch spiritual reality; he will immediately say amen. When others who have touched spiritual reality touch him, they will also have an inward response and an amen. This is the meaning of Psalms 42:7, which says, "Deep calls unto deep." We can say that reality invokes others to touch reality. We will give a few concrete examples in the following pages to explain what spiritual reality is.

Example One

The Lord told Nicodemus, "Truly, truly, I say to you, Unless one is born of water and the Spirit, he cannot enter into the kingdom of God" (John 3:5). Paul wrote to the saints in Rome, "Or are you ignorant that all of us who have been baptized into Christ Jesus have been baptized into His death? We have been buried therefore with Him through baptism into His death, in order that just as Christ was raised from the dead through the glory of the Father, so also we might walk in newness of life. For if we have grown together with Him in the likeness of His death, indeed we will also be in the likeness of His resurrection" (Rom. 6:3-5). Both the Lord Jesus and Paul spoke of the reality of baptism.

However, some only view this matter from the physical point of view. Their eyes see only water. They say that once a man is washed in the water, he is regenerated. They have not touched the spiritual reality. Some tackle the subject with their mind. They realize that water alone cannot regenerate a person. Therefore, they assert that the baptisms of some are real and inward, and that these ones can enter God's kingdom. However, the baptisms of others are false and outward, and these ones cannot enter God's kingdom. They have not touched the spiritual reality either.

The baptism that the Lord mentioned to Nicodemus was a reality. The baptism that Paul saw was a burial with the Lord, with the result of one walking in newness of life. To the Colossian believers, he spoke of being "buried together with Him in baptism, in which also you were raised together with Him" (Col. 2:12). Paul saw that baptism and burial are one and the same thing, and he also saw that baptism and resurrection are one and the same thing. Paul knew what it meant to be buried with the Lord and to be raised up together with the Lord. He did not only see the baptismal water. Nor was he merely concerned with whether a baptism was true or false. He was speaking of the reality of baptism.

Brothers and sisters, if you see that baptism is a reality, you will spontaneously know what baptism is. In your mind, there will not be a distinction between real and false baptism, and there will be no question of an outward or inward baptism. You will see that baptism is being buried with the Lord and being raised up together with Him. Once you see this reality, you will exclaim, "Baptism is a great matter. It is too real and too all-inclusive." Once a man sees this reality, false things can no longer remain in him. If a man says, "I have been baptized, but I wish that I could be buried and raised up together with the Lord," he has not touched spiritual reality. Baptism is one thing to him, and burial and resurrection are another. Yet those who know spiritual reality know what burial is and what resurrection is. They know that baptism is burial and resurrection. Baptism is these very things to him.

Brothers and sisters, have you seen this? A man will never see spiritual things if he tries to see them with his physical eyes. A man will never understand spiritual things if he tries to understand them with his mind. All spiritual things have their realities. Once we touch the realities, all problems will go away.

Example Two

The same is true with the breaking of bread. On the night the Lord Jesus was betrayed, "Jesus took bread and blessed it, and He broke it and gave it to the disciples and said, Take, eat; this is My body. And He took a cup and gave thanks, and He gave it to them, saying, Drink of it, all of you, for this is My blood of the covenant, which is being poured out for many for the forgiveness of sins. But I say to you, I shall by no means drink of this product of the vine…" (Matt. 26:26-29a). Some look at this from a physical point of view and say that once the bread and the cup are blessed, the bread changes its nature, becoming the Lord's flesh, and the vine product changes its substance, becoming the Lord's blood. Some look at this from an intellectual point of view and argue that the bread and the wine have not changed in substance; rather, they are merely representations. The bread represents the Lord's body, and the vine product represents the Lord's blood. But the emphasis in the Word of God is not on a change in substance or on the matter of representation, it is on a spiritual reality. When we "take, eat," there is a spiritual reality behind it. When we "drink of it, all of you," there is a spiritual reality to it. He said, "This is My body." He did not say, "This represents My body." He said, "This is My blood of the covenant." Following this, He said, "I shall by no means drink of this product of the vine." This means that the product of the vine did not turn into blood, and neither was it a representation of the blood. In speaking of the bread and the cup, the Lord's emphasis was on the spiritual reality. In the eyes of the Lord, there are no representations, and there is no change of substance. Paul said the same thing. "The cup of blessing which we bless, is it not the fellowship of the blood of Christ? The bread which we break, is it not the fellowship of the body of Christ?" (1 Cor. 10:16). It was bread, yet Paul recognized it as the Body of Christ. It was a cup, yet he recognized it as the blood of Christ. This shows that in Paul's mind, there was no such thing as a representation or a change in substance. These things were a spiritual reality to him. Following this, Paul said, "Seeing that we, who are many, are one bread, one body" (v. 17, ASV). He could not have said this if he had not touched the spiritual reality. When a man says a fact, it is stated as a fact. If it is a parable, it is stated as a parable. If it is a plain narration, it is presented as a plain narration, and if it is a figure of speech, it is explained as a figure of speech. But here Paul was different. The phrase "we, who are many" is a direct narration, while "are one bread" is a figure of speech. In one sentence, he put a direct narration together with a figure of speech. This is because with Paul, "we, who are many" is a fact, and "are one bread, one body" is also a fact. To him, the spiritual reality is so real that after he said, "we, who are many," he followed with the words "are one bread, one body." He was not thinking about the grammatical structure or the syntax. Here was a person who truly knew the Lord. When he took the bread, he was truly partaking of the Body of Christ. He forgot about the bread, and was touching the spiritual reality. When he took the cup, he was truly partaking of the blood of Christ. He forgot the vine product, and was touching the spiritual reality. Language was no longer a problem to him, and doctrine was no longer a problem to him because he touched the reality.

Example Three

The church is an even more interesting subject. When some people mention the church, they try to differentiate between the true church and the false church. But the Lord said to Peter, "And I also say to you that you are Peter, and upon this rock I will build My church, and the gates of Hades shall not prevail against it. I will give to you the keys of the kingdom of the heavens, and whatever you bind on the earth shall have been bound in the heavens, and whatever you loose on the earth shall have been loosed in the heavens" (Matt. 16:18-19). This is what the church is in the Lord's mind. In the Lord's mind, the church is always real; there is no such thing as a false church. Not only is this true with the universal church, but this is even true with the local churches. He says, "Moreover if your brother sins against you, go, reprove him between you and him alone. If he hears you, you have gained your brother. But if he does not hear you, take with

you one or two more, that by the mouth of two or three wit-
nesses every word may be established. And if he refuses to
hear them, tell it to the church; and if he refuses to hear the
church also, let him be to you just like the Gentile and the tax
collector. Truly I say to you, Whatever you bind on the earth
shall have been bound in heaven, and whatever you loose on
the earth shall have been loosed in heaven" (18:15-18). In the
Lord's mind, when the church says that a brother is right, he
is right, and when the church says that a brother is wrong,
he is wrong. When we read this, it is easy for us to ask the
question: What if the judgment of the church is wrong? But
when the Lord spoke these words, He was talking about the
reality of the church. If the judgment is wrong, it must not
have come from reality, and it must not be of the Holy Spirit,
but of man. In the Lord's mind, the church is a reality. Anything outside this reality has no place in the Lord's mind at
all.

When Paul spoke of the church in his Epistles, he said
that it is called, it is holy, and it is the house of God (Rom. 1:7;
1 Cor. 1:2; Eph. 2:22). The apostle John said the same thing as
Paul concerning the church. The seven churches in Asia had
many failures, but John still called them the churches. The
Lord Jesus also said, "The seven lampstands are the seven
churches" (Rev. 1:4, 20).

In the eyes of the apostles, the seven lampstands are the
seven churches because the church is a reality. In the eyes
of the apostles, the matter of a false church did not exist,
because the church is a reality. This does not mean that there
are no false churches in this world. But it does mean that
if one does not see the reality of the church, his eyes surely
will see something wrong. Those who look at the church outwardly will say that there is only the real church, and those
who look at the church mentally will say that there are real
churches and false churches. But in the eyes of those who
have touched the spiritual reality, the church is spiritual, and
all other questions have no ground at all.

I would like to mention one thing concerning the practice
of the Body life. The Body life is not acting according to certain rules. When one touches the spiritual reality, he touches

the church, and his actions will be the move of the Body and not independent moves. Suppose you have to do something. Practicing the Body life does not mean that you invite all the brothers and sisters to discuss it and that you go through the procedure in a very proper way. It is when you fellowship with other brothers and sisters (irrespective of the number) and touch the reality that there is the Body life. If you have not touched the spiritual reality, even when there is unanimous consent by the whole congregation, you only have opinions of the flesh and not the Body life. Only those who have touched the spiritual reality can live the Body life. The record in Acts 15 shows us what the Body life is. There was a gathering to discuss the question of circumcision for the Gentiles. Finally, James made a decision that was of the Holy Spirit. When they wrote the letter, they said, "For it seemed good to the Holy Spirit and to us" (v. 28). The decision was of the Holy Spirit. It touched the spiritual reality. Although the words were by James, "the apostles and the elders with the whole church" (v. 22) could say amen to them and resolve to carry the matter out. This is the Body life. Only when one touches the reality in the Holy Spirit can he live out the Body life. The right procedure does not bring in the Body life. One must touch the reality before there can be the Body life.

We must realize that all spiritual living and all spiritual teachings have their realities before the Lord. If a man has not touched the reality, there is no spiritual value to expounding the doctrine clearly. If a man has not touched the reality of the church, even if he mentions the church in every other sentence, he is still in darkness and pride, and he is deceiving himself. If a man touches the spiritual reality, his living will be real and organic. It will not be superficial or in letters.

One amazing thing is that a person who touches reality knows if others have not touched or entered into it as soon as he comes in contact with them. Once he meets a person who acts according to his mind, the law, or outward regulations, he will know immediately that such a person has not touched the reality. There is one thing before the Lord, which the Bible calls *reality*. Once a person touches this reality, he will be delivered from doctrines, formalities, human thoughts, and human ways. Baptism, the breaking of bread, or the church are all realities to him; they are no longer rituals or doctrines.

Example Four

Let us consider the matter of worship again. John 4 tells us that "God is Spirit, and those who worship Him must worship in spirit and truthfulness" (v. 24). We have pointed out previously that the word "truthfulness" can be translated as "reality." The emphasis is the spirit, but it also mentions reality. Those who worship God must worship with their spirit. Anything that is of the spirit is real, and anything that is not of the spirit is not real. One does not worship God by the emotions, the feelings, or the mind. To worship God, one must be in spirit and in reality. Otherwise, one cannot touch spiritual reality. What is reality? When the spirit touches God, there is reality; when the spirit does not touch God, there is no reality. Anything that is of the spirit is real, and anything that is not of the spirit is not real. Formalistic worship is, of course, not up to the standard. But the so-called spiritual worship is, at times, unworthy of an amen. One may not be able to put his finger on the problem, but there is a feeling that it is not the real thing. Then there are those who are truly worshipping God; they may not say anything. However you can say amen, because you have touched something real in them; you have touched the reality in them.

Example Five

Thanksgiving and praise are good things. But many thanksgivings and praises are ritualistic. They are not what the Bible describes as reality. Brothers and sisters, have you had the experience in which someone was thanking and praising but there was not an amen within you? In fact, you felt quite cold within. It seemed that the more the person praised, the colder you became. Sometimes a person encounters a problem, and he continues to thank and praise the Lord in a loud way, acting as if there is no problem at all. Is this good? It seems good. But the more he praises and thanks the Lord, the more you cannot say amen. You do not understand why. But something within you says, "It is good to thank and praise the

Lord, but this kind of thanksgiving and praise is not genuine. It is not the reality." Some people seem to be unconcerned about their problems; they fill their mouths with joyful and happy thanksgivings and praises. But within, you feel that there is something wrong, that it is not right, and that it is not the reality. You may meet another brother who is not as loud as the first one in thanking and praising the Lord. He may not appear as joyful and may, in fact, show some sadness in his face. But the strange thing is that when he thanks and praises the Lord in a soft way, you can say amen. You feel that it is right, that it is the real thing, and that he has touched the reality.

Example Six

Take prayer as another example. I will not mention formalistic prayers. Seemingly zealous prayers and long prayers often do not strike an amen in others. On the contrary, the more these prayers are offered, the more others become cold. This is because the prayer has not touched any spiritual reality. Luke 18 speaks of two persons praying in the temple. The prayer of the tax collector who "beat his breast, saying, God, be propitiated to me, the sinner!" (v. 13) touched others. But the prayer of the self-justifying Pharisee who praised God loudly did not touch others. This is because one was praying to God, while the other was only praying "to himself" (v. 11). Many prayers that are prayers to oneself do not strike any amen. On the contrary, they make others sick. A real prayer may be short in words and may even be inarticulate, but when one prays such a prayer, he touches reality. He touches the depth of others' beings, and others can respond with a spontaneous amen.

Example Seven

Another matter is the blood of the Lord Jesus cleansing our conscience. Physically speaking, this is an impossible thing. When the Lord Jesus was crucified on the cross, could anyone take the blood which was shed and sprinkle it on himself to cleanse his conscience? No. The Holy Spirit is the Executor of all spiritual things. When the Holy Spirit cleanses our conscience with the Lord's blood, He is cleansing us with the spiritual reality of the blood rather than the physical blood. Something is real only when it is in the Holy Spirit. When we touch the reality in the Holy Spirit, we touch life. But if all we touch are doctrines, the result is death, and we will not have life.

Example Eight

Romans 6 says that our old man has been crucified with Christ (v. 6). This is a fact. Some Christians say, "I know that my old man is crucified, but I do not know why my old man is still living today." The reason for this is that they have touched a doctrine; they have not touched the spiritual reality. We must realize that if a doctrine is in letters and not in the Holy Spirit, we will not receive any life even if we know all about it. If we merely touch the doctrines of salvation, justification, and sanctification, what we have are merely letters, and they are dead. A doctrine must be in the Holy Spirit before it can become a spiritual reality. When we touch the spiritual reality, we touch life, and it is living and fresh.

A person may seemingly deliver a very spiritual sermon. Yet what he says stifles others because he has not said the real thing itself. When a man touches reality, what he says will be real. It is reality that causes others to touch reality. Otherwise, even if there are extensive quotations and references, and even if all the logic is right, those who know reality will still say that it is not reality.

Example Nine

Another matter is the knowledge of Christ. Those who know Christ according to outward appearance do not really know Him. The only real knowledge is the knowledge in reality. When the Lord Jesus was on earth, men seemed to touch Him, but actually they did not touch Him. They seemed to know the Lord Jesus, but actually they did not know Him. Their knowledge was outward and superficial. Those who truly knew the Lord Jesus were the ones who touched the reality. Their knowledge was in the spirit. We must consider a little more from the Bible concerning this point because this is a very basic experience.

When the Lord Jesus was on earth, men knew Him in two ways. One was knowledge according to appearance, and the other was inward knowledge. Let us first consider the meaning of knowing Him according to outward appearance.

The Jews knew the Lord Jesus according to His outward appearance. They held on to their presumptuous attitude from the very beginning. They said, "Is not this Jesus, the son of Joseph, whose father and mother we know?" (John 6:42). They were very confident. Since they knew His father and mother, they thought that they knew Him as well. When the Lord Jesus came into His own country, they said, "Is not this the carpenter, the son of Mary, and brother of James and Joses and Judas and Simon? And are not His sisters here with us?" (Mark 6:3). They knew not only the Lord's parents, but His brothers and sisters as well. But did they really know the Lord Jesus? No, they did not know Him. Although they knew the Lord's parents, they did not know the Lord Jesus. Although they knew the Lord's brothers and sisters, they did not know Him. They judged who the Lord was by His outward appearance, and they did not touch the reality.

Another group of people knew the Lord a little deeper than the Jews. But they still did not know Him in an inward way. When the Lord was in Caesarea Philippi, He asked the disciples, "Who do men say that the Son of Man is?" They said, "Some, John the Baptist; and others, Elijah; and still others, Jeremiah or one of the prophets" (Matt. 16:13-14). This was much more advanced than the knowledge of the Jews. Some said that the Lord was Elijah. Elijah was a powerful prophet; he can be considered as a symbol of power. The Lord Jesus was indeed an Elijah; He was a most powerful prophet. Others said that the Lord was Jeremiah. Jeremiah was a weeping prophet; he can be considered as a symbol of emotion. The Lord Jesus was indeed a Jeremiah, one who was full of emotion. When He rebuked the hypocritical scribes and Pharisees, He repeated eight times, "Woe to you" (23:13-16, 23, 25, 27, 29). When He saw some selling oxen and sheep and doves, and the moneychangers sitting there, He poured out the money of the moneychangers and overturned their tables (John 2:15). He was truly an Elijah. When He was with the tax collectors and the sinners, He feasted with them (Matt. 9:10). When He sat down in the house of Simon, He allowed a woman to weep over His feet (Luke 7:37-38). When He saw Mary weeping and the Jews who came with her also weeping, He sighed in His spirit, and wept also! (John 11:33, 35). He was truly a Jeremiah. But whether others called Him Elijah or Jeremiah, this knowledge was still outward knowledge.

The disciples' knowledge of the Lord Jesus in the beginning was outward knowledge; they did not have an inward knowledge of Him. Men like Thomas and Philip were with the Lord for a long time. Humanly speaking, they should have known the Lord. Yet they did not know Him. The Lord clearly said, "Where I am going you know the way." Yet Thomas said to the Lord, "Lord, we do not know where You are going; how can we know the way?" (John 14:4-5). The Lord clearly said, "If you had known Me, you would have known My Father also; and henceforth you know Him and have seen Him." But Philip said to Him, "Lord, show us the Father and it is sufficient for us" (vv. 7-8). The Jesus that Thomas knew was only a Nazarene; Thomas did not know the Jesus of life. The Jesus that Philip knew was only a Nazarene; Philip did not know that He was the embodiment of the Father. Although Philip and Thomas were with the Lord, their knowledge of Him was only outward; they did not touch the reality.

Although the disciples knew the Lord a little better than the Jews, they did not know what kind of Lord He was. The Lord was with them for a long time, but they still did not know Him. They saw the Lord with their own eyes, heard Him with their own ears, and touched Him with their own hands. But they still did not know Him. This shows us that in knowing the Lord, one needs an organ that is sharper than the outward eyes, clearer than the outward ears, and more sensitive than the outward hands. With Christ, there is a reality, and this reality cannot be discerned by outward appearance.

One day Peter had inward knowledge. When the Lord asked, "Who do you say that I am?", Simon Peter answered, "You are the Christ, the Son of the living God." Immediately, the Lord said, "Blessed are you, Simon Barjona, because flesh and blood has not revealed this to you, but My Father who is in the heavens" (Matt. 16:15-17). The Lord meant, "You have been following Me for so long, yet your knowledge in the past was wrong. However, your knowledge today is a blessed one, because flesh and blood has not revealed it to you, but My Father who is in the heavens has revealed it to you." This knowledge was real.

If a man does not have the revelation, even if he can eat, drink, walk, and dwell together with the Lord Jesus, he will still not know who He is. A knowledge that is void of revelation is a knowledge of an outward Christ, a historical Christ. This is knowing Him according to the flesh. The only kind of knowledge of Christ that is real and inward is the one that Peter acquired through revelation.

Paul said, "So then we, from now on, know no one according to the flesh; even though we have known Christ according to the flesh, yet now we know Him so no longer" (2 Cor. 5:16). When Paul knew Christ according to the flesh, he was fearless in attacking the name of Jesus of Nazareth and in persecuting the Lord's disciples and in punishing them (Acts 26:9-11). But after God revealed His Son in his spirit, he began to announce the faith which formerly he ravaged (Gal. 1:16, 23). He became a different man. His knowledge touched the spiritual reality, and he no longer knew Christ according to the flesh.

Mark records the story of a woman with a flow of blood for twelve years. "When she heard the things concerning Jesus, she came up in the crowd behind Him and touched His garment....And immediately the fountain of her blood was dried up, and she knew in her body that she was cured of the affliction." What did the Lord feel? He said, "Who touched My garments?" The disciples said, "You see the crowd pressing upon You and You say, Who touched Me?" (5:27-31). Here we see two groups of people—those who touched the Lord and those who pressed upon Him. Those who pressed upon Him could only contact Christ in the flesh. Only those who touched Him touched Christ in reality. The Lord did not seem to feel those who pressed upon Him. But the minute someone touched Him, He felt it. How sad it is that there were so many who pressed upon Him and only one who touched Him! The Lord said, "But in truth I say to you, There were many widows in Israel in the days of Elijah, when the sky was shut up for three years and six months, when a great famine came over all the land; and to none of them was Elijah sent, except to the city of Sarepta of Sidon, to a woman who was a widow. And there were many lepers in Israel during the time of Elisha the prophet, and none of them were cleansed, except Naaman the Syrian" (Luke 4:25-27). This is similar to the story of the woman who was healed of the flowing of blood. It is not a question of distance or time. It is a question of who is pressing upon Him and who is touching the reality. If a man has not touched reality, he will not change even if he manages to come before the Lord and press close upon Him.

Those who know Christ according to the flesh never actually know Him. One must have revelation before he can know Him. We cannot know Christ according to our outward senses of sight, sound, or touch. The knowledge of Christ is something that the Holy Spirit imparts to us. If a man does not have the Holy Spirit, he does not know the reality of Christ. In the eyes of God, if a man does not have the Holy Spirit, he has not touched the reality of the Lord Jesus even if he has memorized the Lord's history and even if he has pressed upon Him, heard His voice, knelt before Him, and prayed to Him.

The Lord said, "The words which I have spoken to you are spirit and are life" (John 6:63). Hence, once a man touches the Holy Spirit, he will surely have life. It is impossible for a man to touch the Holy Spirit without receiving life. Anything that is of the Holy Spirit is of life. If a man touches reality, he receives life. But this is where the problem lies: many people receive their knowledge of the Lord from books, while others receive it from other men. Whether they receive it by reading or hearing from others, they may not be touching the Lord Himself. The Christ that one acquires through reading or hearing cannot be compared to the real Christ. The real Christ can only be known in the Holy Spirit; there is no other way to know Him.

Many Christians are discouraged at times. It seems as if

their faith avails nothing. They say, "I have been listening to messages for many years. I know very much, but none of the things I know are useful and workable." This is because they have not touched reality. If a man tries to touch Christ with his fleshly hands, he can never expect any result. Power did not go out to those who pressed upon Him. It only went out to the woman who touched Him. Many pressed upon Him but did not touch Him. However, one touched Him. Whether or not our faith works depends on whether or not we have touched reality.

We must realize that the Christ in the flesh can be touched by fleshly hands, seen by fleshly eyes, and heard by fleshly ears. But the Christ in the Holy Spirit can only be touched when a man is in the spirit. To touch the Christ in the flesh is different from touching the Christ in the Spirit. When the Lord Jesus was on earth, there was already a difference between outward and inward knowledge. The same difference exists today with our knowledge of Him. The real issue is how we know Christ. If we know Christ in a real way through the Spirit and touch the spiritual reality of Christ, we will have an inward knowledge, even though we may not be able to articulate or explain it. Once there is inward knowledge, all doubts will be gone. We need to ask the Lord to give us true knowledge, true seeing, so that we will know the Lord, not according to ourselves or to the revelation of flesh and blood, but according to the revelation of the Father who is in the heavens.

Example Ten

It is right for brothers to forgive brothers. But sometimes we find a brother forgiving someone who has offended him in a very loud, forceful, and deliberate way. He has forgiven generously, but we inwardly feel that something is not right; it seems that the forgiveness is too deliberate; it does not feel like the real thing. This is because he has not touched reality. We may meet another brother who was hurt by someone. He is sad and not rejoicing. Yet he believes that God can never be wrong and that he ought to forgive from his heart. He does not proclaim loudly with his mouth that he is forgiving. He does not show others that he is forgiving. He does not seem as unconcerned as the first one. Yet in the end, he forgives his brother. One senses that this brother is not performing; he is forgiving. He has touched the spiritual reality.

Example Eleven

Humility should be something that leaves a good impression in the mind of others. But the humility of some Christians makes others feel that they are striving to be humble. They say with their mouth that they can do nothing, yet one has the feeling that this is "self-chosen lowliness" and "self-imposed...lowliness" (Col. 2:18, 23). It gives one the feeling that what is being expressed is not humility itself. If it is outright pride, one can still call it by its name. But it is hard to pinpoint what this kind of humility really is. One cannot say that it is pride, but neither can one say that it is humility. Outwardly, it looks like humility, but actually it is far from the reality of it. Another brother may not be striving as hard to be humble. But a little remark by him and a spontaneous expression from him exposes others' pride immediately. Others feel ashamed of their pride; they feel that if anyone is qualified to be proud, this brother should be the one because he has something to be proud of. Yet this brother considers others better than himself, and he seeks their help in a very unpretentious way. This brother has touched the reality of humility.

Example Twelve

Let us consider the example of love again. First Corinthians 13 gives us a clear picture of love. "And if I dole out all my possessions to feed others, and if I deliver up my body that I may boast..." (v. 3). Humanly speaking, it is hard to find this kind of love in the world. We can say that there is no greater love than this. Yet Paul continued by saying, "...but do not have love, I profit nothing" (v. 3). This means that it is possible to be without love even when one doles out all his possessions to feed others and delivers up his body that he may boast. In other words, unless he is touching the reality in the Spirit, he merely has outward behavior. It is possible for a brother to dole out all of his possessions to feed others and deliver up his body yet, at the same time, be without love. However, if a brother "gives to one of these little ones only a cup of cold water to drink...he shall by no means lose his reward" (Matt. 10:42). The basic question is not how much or how little one does, but whether or not he has touched reality. The only thing that is real is touching reality through the Spirit of the Lord.

We must see that in God's eyes we cannot do more than what we are. Some people's love is great, but it makes others doubt whether the love is real or false. Some Christians have such a great "love" that they seem to be void of any human feelings. It makes others put a question mark on their love. In reading 2 Corinthians, we realize that Paul was misunderstood, slandered, and afflicted with pain and hardship; however, he overcame these things. His victory was the victory of a man, not the victory of an angel. He genuinely overcame, and he was a genuine man. He was a genuine man, and his victory was a genuine victory. Through the Spirit of God, he touched something real. When we read his writings, we cannot help but bow our head and say that here is a man who is not too distant from us. We can almost touch such a man. We feel that he was not among the ranks of Michael or Gabriel; he was not a person living among the cherubim. We feel that he was one we can understand. This is because he had the spiritual reality, and when we touch such a man, we touch life.

CONDUCT AND REALITY

We must remember that in God's eyes, there is something called reality. The problem with many Christians is that they try to do something to make things real. However, what is expressed is, in fact, not reality. Many Christians try to manufacture a kind of "reality" before the Lord. They try to imitate and copy. But God does not require us to imitate; He only wants the reality, the real thing, to be manifested through us. What we generate by ourselves is artificial and fabricated; it is not the reality. We must see the vanity of acting according to doctrines. At the most, a man who does this has outward conduct; he does not have the real thing, and what he has is not the reality.

Therefore, we have to learn to live before the Lord in what we *are*. We must ask God to help us so that we would touch the reality behind all spiritual things. Many times, we are very close to falsehood because we know too much doctrine; we walk according to doctrines instead of walking according to the leading of the Spirit of God. Anytime we walk according to doctrines, we cannot touch reality.

A brother said the following when relating his experience: "Once a brother offended me very much. He came to me and said something to me. I responded, 'Brother, it does not matter. It is all right.' But within me I said, 'This is not right. He does this kind of thing all the time. He does it not only to me, but to many people as well.' I had the thought of saying something harsh to him. But if I said something harsh, he would think that I was an unforgiving person, and he might be hurt. Of course, if I shook his hand and invited him for a meal, I would be seen as practicing brotherly love. While I was thinking about this, a strong urge within me said, 'You have to tell him the truth today, and you have to show him that he is wrong.' I struggled for a quarter of an hour. In the end I spoke the truth to him." Sometimes rebukes are more valuable than handshakes. We can have an outward gentleness and win the praises of others, but this kind of thing has no spiritual value at all before God. The question is whether our conduct issues from dead doctrines or from the leading of the Spirit. Our brother truly loved his brother from his heart. But the question is not merely one of the heart, but whether or not there is the spiritual reality.

A Christian once argued with his family. One member in the family was very fierce and slapped him on the face. At that instant, he remembered the words of Matthew 5, which say, "Whoever slaps you on your right cheek, turn to him the other also" (v. 39). He thought that since he was a Christian, he should behave like a Christian. Therefore, he turned his other cheek. After he did this, he could not sleep well for two nights. As far as his conduct was concerned, he had acted according to the Scripture. But he was so furious that he could not sleep well for two nights. This means that he had not touched the spiritual reality. His conduct was not life; it was not the real thing.

Many Christians feel that they have one shortcoming: they cannot differentiate between the real thing and the false thing; they cannot tell what is of God and what is not of God. As far as their spiritual experience is concerned, they cannot tell the difference because they have not touched the spiritual reality. If they have touched reality, their eyes will discern what is not reality right away. The power of discernment comes from what one sees. If you have touched the spiritual reality in one matter, no one will be able to deceive you in that matter anymore. A genuinely saved Christian has touched spiritual reality at least in the matter of salvation. It is not that easy for anyone to deceive him in the matter of salvation. In the same way, if he has touched the reality in any other matter, he will spontaneously feel the difference whenever there is the absence of reality in that particular matter. Once he touches something unreal, an inexplicable power within will repel the unreal thing; something within will tell him immediately that this is not the real thing.

We are easily deceived because we often deceive ourselves. Those who deceive themselves are easily deceived by others. If one is blind about himself, he will be blind about others. Whenever we know ourselves, we know others. We cannot know others if we do not know ourselves. If we have passed through God's dealings and if we know ourselves, we will spontaneously know others. Once we are touched and dealt with by God in a certain matter, once we touch something real, and once we know the way God's Spirit moves within, we will know immediately when we touch a person whether he acts by himself or by the Spirit of God. Spiritual discernment comes only after one has touched spiritual reality. Those who have not touched reality can only deceive two kinds of people—themselves and those whose spiritual condition is the same as theirs. They cannot deceive those who know what is of the Spirit and what living in the Spirit is. Even more, they cannot deceive the church. They may think that they are spiritual, but the strange thing is that the church will never say amen to them. We must realize that whenever the church cannot say amen, we have to confess our sins. If the brothers and sisters cannot respond with an amen, it means that there is falsehood and the absence of reality.

Many brothers and sisters are vexing and burdening the church not only by their sins, but by their "good" conduct. Sin can easily be detected, but it is not that easy to detect the many kinds of "good" conduct that originate from man himself; it is not that easy to detect that they are far from God and far from spiritual reality. Many Christians have not touched any spiritual reality. What they do has nothing to do with reality. Yet they still think that they have the reality. This is truly a vexation and a burden. We believe that whenever one touches reality, the result is life, and whenever one does not touch reality, the result is death. Some people do certain things, touch life, and cause others to touch life also. Some people do certain things and feel quite happy about what they have done, yet others do not touch life, and they are not edified. Those who touch life do not appreciate these kinds of works; rather, they dislike them. These works originate from the self and do not bring in life; rather, they bring in death.

We must learn to live in the Spirit. Otherwise, we may accomplish many "good" works without touching any spiritual reality at all. What does it mean to live in the Spirit? It means that we do not do things by ourselves. Doing things by ourselves is being of the flesh, and being of the flesh is surely far from spiritual reality. Spiritual reality is something spiritual; it is not fleshly. Simply put, spiritual reality is what one touches through the Holy Spirit. Only what we touch through the Holy Spirit is living and real. Any work that a Christian has apart from the Holy Spirit is not real. His work can never replace the real thing in God's eyes. His work cannot help others and cannot edify himself. May the Lord be merciful to us and may He show us that those who live in the Spirit are the only ones who live in spiritual reality.

SUPPLY AND REALITY

Second Corinthians 4 shows us clearly that where there is

reality, there is the supply. Paul said, "Always bearing about in the body the putting to death of Jesus that the life of Jesus also may be manifested in our body" (v. 10). This shows us that when the death of Jesus is manifested, His life is also manifested. In other words, the life of Jesus is seen in us because the death of Jesus is seen in us. When a group of people knows the death of Jesus, life is made manifest in them. Paul then said, "So then death operates in us, but life in you" (v. 12). In verse 10, he spoke of the manifestation of life. In verse 12 he spoke of the supply of life. When the manifestation is in us, it is life. When the manifestation is in others, it is supply. But the source is the same—the death of Jesus. Therefore, hollow preachings are vain. Preachings that do not touch any reality do not render any supply to the Body of Christ. When the death of Jesus operates in us, the life of Jesus operates in others. This is not a matter of preaching or work, but a matter of the supply of life. Of course, preaching has its use. But if there is no reality behind one's preaching, there will not be the supply of life. When we have the "death of Jesus" in us, the Body of Christ receives the supply. Where there is reality, there is supply. If we do not know what the "death of Jesus" means and if we have not borne the cross in silence, we do not have the supply. Brothers and sisters, we have to remember that as far as spiritual reality is concerned, no work should be "performed" by us. When we pass through something in a real way, the Body of Christ spontaneously receives the supply. On our side, we should know the "death of Jesus," and on the side of the Body of Christ, there will be the supply spontaneously.

Therefore, there is no need for us to tell others that we are forgiving others. There is no need for us to blow the trumpet and tell others that we are loving them. We do not need to draw attention to our bearing of the cross. If we touch reality, spontaneously, others will receive the supply. It does not matter whether or not we know that others are supplied, and it does not matter whether or not we feel it. One fact is certain: "Death operates in us, but life in you."

Our trouble is that we know too many doctrines already. We act merely according to teachings and do not have the

supply of reality. We need to realize that supply is not superficial behavior; supply is the reality. If we know what "the
death of Jesus" means before the Lord, "the life of Jesus" will
operate in the church spontaneously. If it is life, there will be
the supply spontaneously. Supply gives life to others; it is not
an exhibition of our own work. Supply edifies others, rather
than broadcasts our own experience. The most important
thing for us to do is have the supply through possessing the
reality. Every time we pass through "the death of Jesus,"
there will always be some brothers and sisters who receive
the supply of life. There will be no need for us to wait to write
an autobiography before others will receive the supply. As
soon as we receive life from the Lord, the church will have the
supply of life.

We must realize that the help many receive transcends
consciousness and feelings. As long as we have the reality,
others will receive the supply whether or not we feel it. Life is
a fact. Whenever we are truly bearing the cross before the
Lord, the Body of Christ will receive the supply. If we do not
know the meaning of the supply of life, we will not understand what Paul meant when he said, "Death operates in us,
but life in you." Moreover, he told the Colossian saints, "I now
rejoice in my sufferings on your behalf and fill up on my part
that which is lacking of the afflictions of Christ in my flesh
for His Body, which is the church" (Col. 1:24). What is this?
This is the supply of life. If we see that the Body of Christ is
one, spontaneously there will be the supply. This is why Paul
was able to suffer for the sake of the Body of Christ, and this
is why he could fill up the lack of the afflictions of Christ in
his flesh. If we do not see that the Body of Christ is one, we
will not realize how the lack of the afflictions of Christ is
being filled up.

May the Lord open our eyes to see that the Body is one.
Those who truly see that the Body is one will see that everything they have has been received (1 Cor. 4:7). Everything we
have is received; everything we have is a supply to others. The
reality that we alone touch before God is a supply to the
whole Body. The supply of the Body transcends any physical
contact. Paul told the church in Corinth, "For I, on my part,

though being absent in the body but present in the spirit, have already judged, as if being present" (5:3). Paul touched the reality of the Body. Therefore, he could say that he was present with them in his spirit, as if he was present with them in his body. This is not a wish. This is touching the reality. If we see that the Body of Christ is one, our spirit will be with the Body, and this is supply. This supply transcends words, transcends work, and transcends all physical contact. If we know God and are in contact with Him, all of our experiences will become the riches of the Body.

It is a pity that many Christians are still living in outward appearances! There seems to be a supply only when they work, but this supply stops once their work stops. When they open their mouths, they appear to be the best servants of God. But when they do not open their mouths, they are no longer the best servants of God. When others understand them, they can render others the supply. But when they are misunderstood, they cannot render the supply. They have not touched the spiritual reality before the Lord. This is the reason that they cannot render the supply of life to the Body of Christ. One brother may be in the company of others, and he may only open his mouth for five minutes in three hours, yet others receive his supply. The Body of Christ is a fact; one does not receive the supply only when there is the shaking of hands or face-to-face conversations. When a man experiences something before the Lord, and when he receives the "death of Jesus" from God's hand, he has supplied the Body of Christ already. Therefore, brothers and sisters, we supply the church with our inward knowledge of the Lord. We do not have to consciously do something to supply others. We do not have to intentionally do something to supply others. We supply others spontaneously. Those who have not touched reality cannot supply others. Only those who have touched reality will supply others. There is no way to fabricate anything. In Paul's experience, the supply to the Body of Christ is a reality; it is not an act. If we have passed through something in a real way before the Lord, and if there is the real thing in us, we will supply the church spontaneously. As long as we have the real experience, the church will spontaneously receive the benefit.

Paul's word was quite peculiar. It would be easy to understand him if he had said that the death of Jesus operated in him and the life of Jesus also operated in him. But he said that the death of Jesus operated in him, and that as a result, the life of Jesus operated in others. It would be difficult for anyone who does not know the Body of Christ to understand this word. Since the Body is one, what operates in me spontaneously operates in others. This is life, and this is supply. If we see this, we will rejoice. Everything that the members receive from the Head is found in the Body. We are all enjoying the same Body. Brothers and sisters, if we touch this reality, we will not feel that the church is poor or in desolation. Of course, we admit that outwardly speaking, the church does manifest a condition of poverty and desolation. We admit that, outwardly speaking, individual Christians have failed and individual Christian groups have failed. But whenever we touch the reality of the church, we will say that the church is not poor and not in desolation. The riches of the church are not diminished through the failure of individual Christians and individual groups. Day by day, everything that the members receive from the Head is supplied to the church. Paul touched the spiritual reality. As a consequence, he could rebuke the church in Corinth on the one hand, and supply it on the other hand.

Ephesians 4:13 says, "Until we all arrive at the oneness of the faith and of the full knowledge of the Son of God, at a full-grown man, at the measure of the stature of the fullness of Christ." It is difficult to understand this according to our mind or according to outward appearance. Outwardly speaking, it seems as if the oneness of the faith is far away. It is difficult to say when the church will arrive at this. But when we touch the spiritual reality, we will feel that these questions no longer exist. We will know that the church is one in the eyes of God and that it has never been divided. Once we touch reality, all outward problems will go away. If we have not seen the reality, we will not have the supply. Once we see the reality, the supply to others will begin. Hence, supply is based on the experience of the cross, and it is also based on one's contact with the reality of the Body.

We have to realize that the supply of the word is also based on what we have already imparted to the church in life. Brothers and sisters, if what we speak is what we have already given to the church, the Holy Spirit will testify to our words. But if what we speak is not something that we have before the Lord, the Holy Spirit will not testify to the words. If we have imparted a certain matter to the church in life and then speak about that certain matter, others will receive the help from our words. But if our words merely provide others with clearer thoughts and more knowledge, we will only have fruits of the tree of the knowledge of good and evil. The food of the church is life; only the supply of life can be food to the church. The question is not what we can give to others, but what we have already given to the church. What have we contributed to the real church? What can we say is our contribution when we stand before that church? If we have not touched reality, we will have nothing to supply to others. Spiritual things and the reality behind the words supply the church.

Some Christians consider the Body of Christ to be an illustration. They do not see the reality of the Body. As a result they have no way to become a supply to others. If you do not see the Body, there is no way that you can be a supply. If it is the Body, the mouth's eating will be the Body's eating, the eyes' seeing will be the Body's seeing, and the ears' hearing will be the Body's hearing. One member receiving something is the Body receiving something. No matter which brother or sister, as long as one receives something, the whole Body receives it. We have to see that the Body life is not just a matter of corporate living, but a matter of life. If we do not touch the reality, the church will merely be a doctrine, the Body will merely be an illustration, and we will not receive any supply. Brothers and sisters, we have to remember that we are members of the Body, and we are all one Body. We are not alone. Paul said, "And whether one member suffers, all the members suffer with it; or one member is glorified, all the members rejoice with it" (1 Cor. 12:26). Was he speaking vain words, or is this a reality? Paul was a person who had Body-consciousness. If he had not touched the reality of the

Body, he could not have said such a word. May God grant us to touch the source, and may He grant us to touch reality, so that we can supply the church in a spontaneous way.

QUESTIONS AND REALITY

If we do not see any spiritual reality, we will have many questions. Suppose you have heard a great deal about a person but have never seen him. When you meet someone who knows this person, surely you will ask all kinds of questions about him. But there is one person in this world whom you know very well and about whom you have no need to ask anyone. This person is yourself. You yourself are a reality that you know very well. Suppose you enter a house that you have never been to before. You will have to ask how many rooms there are or how big are the windows. But if you have moved into the house, you no longer need to ask these kinds of questions. You do not have to ask about anything that you are clear about. If you are living in reality, you will not need to ask many questions. If a man does not know the Body of Christ, he will ask what the Body of Christ is. But if he knows what the Body of Christ is, he no longer will have to ask any questions.

In spiritual matters, we can only clarify things to the extent that a person no longer has problems spiritually; we cannot clarify things to the extent that a person no longer has questions mentally. Take the case of the preaching of the gospel. Our gospel can only make others believe in a clear way; it cannot make others understand in a clear way. When Philip told Nathanael that he had met the One of whom Moses in the law, and the prophets, wrote, Nathanael said, "Can anything good be from Nazareth?" But after the Lord said, "Before Philip called you, while you were under the fig tree, I saw you," Nathanael touched reality, and he spontaneously confessed, "You are the Son of God; You are the King of Israel" (John 1:45-49). He touched reality, and his questions were gone. This is the way spiritual things work. Once a person touches reality, he will be enlightened within, and whether or not he can explain it, he will know it clearly within.

There are many words in the Bible which can easily cause misunderstandings. But if the Holy Spirit goes with these words, a man will touch spiritual reality. Once a man touches spiritual reality, there will no longer be any misunderstandings. Someone said once that misunderstanding is a mark of darkness. This is true. If a man sees reality, he will not have any misunderstanding.

HOW TO ENTER INTO THE REALITY

However, spiritual reality is often just a term to us; we have not entered into the reality itself. We must enter the reality itself before what we have is real to us. How can we enter into spiritual reality? John 16:13 says, "But when He, the Spirit of reality, comes, He will guide you into all the reality." Verse 14 says, "He will glorify Me, for He will receive of Mine and will declare it to you." These two verses tell us that the Holy Spirit will guide us and the Holy Spirit will lead us into all reality.

The two greatest works of the Holy Spirit are His revelation and His discipline. The revelation of the Holy Spirit shows us the spiritual reality, while the discipline of the Holy Spirit leads us, through the ordering in the environment, into all spiritual reality.

Revelation is the basis of all spiritual progress. If a Christian has not received any revelation, he is shallow and superficial in God's eyes no matter how much spiritual knowledge he has or how good he behaves outwardly. It is possible that he has not even taken one step forward. At the same time, if the revelation of the Spirit is not matched with the discipline of the Spirit, the revelation is not complete. We can say that the revelation of the Spirit is the foundation, while the discipline of the Spirit is the building. But this does not mean that there is one period of time when we have the revelation of the Spirit and another period of time when we have the discipline of the Spirit. The discipline of the Spirit is mixed in with the revelation of the Spirit; while He is revealing, He is disciplining, and while He is disciplining, He is also revealing. Therefore, we cannot say that revelation includes the whole of the Christian life, unless we consider discipline as part of the revelation.

We believe that the Son accomplished everything that the Father committed to Him (17:4). We also believe that the Spirit accomplished everything that the Son committed to Him. We believe that no matter how great a spiritual reality is, the Spirit will bring us into that same reality. Nothing that is of Christ is held back from the church. This is not just a question of our experience, but a question of whether the work of the Holy Spirit is a success or a failure. We must remember that just as Christ accomplished everything, the Spirit will accomplish everything. We have to believe in the trustworthiness of the Spirit, and we have to believe in the perfectness of the work of the Spirit.

The goal of the work of the Spirit is to lead us into that which is real, the reality. On the one hand, the Spirit gives us the revelation and brings us into that which is real so that we will see what we are in Christ. On the other hand, the Spirit gives the discipline. It seems that some Christians are lacking in something. It seems that there is very little work and very little constitution of the Spirit in them. It seems that they can hardly help themselves, let alone help others. It seems that they can hardly supply their own needs, let alone supply the needs of others. If a Christian wants to help others, he must allow the Lord's Spirit to lead him into reality. In order to lead him into spiritual reality, the Lord's Spirit will have to lead him into much discipline and trials.

David said, "O God of my righteousness; / You made room for me when I was in straits" (Psa. 4:1). God allowed David to fall into straits in order that he would be enlarged. James 2:5 says, "Listen, my beloved brothers: Did not God choose the poor in the world to be rich in faith and heirs of the kingdom, which He promised to those who love Him?" God chose the poor of this world in order that they could be rich in faith. God has no intention to always leave His children in distress. He has no intention to leave them in poverty all the time. He intends to enlarge His children through straits and enrich them in faith through poverty.

Revelation 21 tells us of the future condition of the church before God. What kind of condition will it be? The New Jerusalem will have "the glory of God. Her light was like a most precious stone, like a jasper stone, as clear as crystal" (v. 11). "And the building work of its wall was jasper; and the city was pure gold, like clear glass. The foundations of the wall of the city were adorned with every precious stone" (vv. 18-19). "And the city lies square, and its length is as great as the breadth. And he measured the city with the reed to a length of twelve thousand stadia; the length and the breadth and the height of it are equal" (v. 16). This shows us the riches and the enlargement of the church when it appears before God one day.

What does it mean to be enlarged? Psalm 4:1 tells us that while one is in straits, God can enlarge him until he can enjoy God. This means that enlargement brings in the enjoyment of God, and that straits will never press one down. Those who see the fourth person walking in the midst of the fiery furnace (Dan. 3:25) are the ones who enjoy God. Such persons are enlarged. Those who are imprisoned and whose feet are secured in the locks, yet still pray and sing hymns of praise to God (Acts 16:24-25), are the ones who enjoy God. Such ones are the enlarged ones. Although the gate of the prison was locked, those who were inside could still enjoy the Lord's presence. These are the enlarged ones.

The Spirit enlarges us through distress. Unfortunately, sometimes when we are in distress, we cannot deliver ourselves out of it. We know that the Lord allowed Job to suffer in order to bring him to the Lord's end (James 5:11). Job indeed reached the Lord's end. But unfortunately, many people end themselves before they reach the Lord's end! Some stumble in their trials while they are being tried. They are in distress, but they are not enlarged. Some murmur against God the minute they are tried; they complain that God is not being fair to them. As a result, they are trapped by their own trials, and they are not enlarged.

Some Christians are not in distress, yet they are very poor. They lack spiritual reality, and what they have is not sufficient for their own use, much less for helping others. However, some Christians are rich, and one cannot fathom their depth or exhaust their measure. When anyone brings their problems to them, they can always render some help. It seems as though no problem is unsolvable before them, and it seems as if no one who goes to them comes away without receiving help. One can only bow his head and thank the Lord for giving such rich ones to the church. Their riches are greater than the problems and poverty of others; they are well able to render the supply. They are rich; therefore, they can render the supply. They are rich because they have touched reality.

Whether or not a church can be the golden lampstand and a testimony depends on how many enlarged believers are in that church. It depends on how many believers are rich in faith, who can supply others. When a friend comes to us at midnight to borrow loaves, and we have nothing to set before him, we can go and knock on our other friend's door (Luke 11:5-6). But sometimes, when others need the loaves, the Lord tells us, "You give them something to eat" (Matt. 14:16). How many loaves do we really have? We can often pray for provisional supplies, and the Lord can grant mercy to us. But provisional prayers cannot replace riches. If we do not have any increase in spiritual riches over a year or even five years, we are indeed in poverty!

What is the reason for our poverty? The reason lies in the lack of discipline from the Spirit and the lack of restrictions of the Spirit. We must remember that every enlarged person has gone through some experiences before the Lord. They have a certain amount of history before the Lord. Their experiences and history become the riches of the church. Many sicknesses are present in order to increase the riches of the church. Many problems are present in order to increase the riches of the church. Many obstacles and hardships are present in order to increase the riches of the church. Many Christians live in peace, yet their end is spiritual poverty. When other brothers and sisters are faced with problems, they cannot understand and render any spiritual help to them. They do not have a history before God, and the Holy Spirit has no opportunity to manifest the reality of Christ through them or to wrought Christ into them. They may have heard many teachings, but teachings cannot replace the work of the Spirit.

With those who do not have the work of the Spirit, the Lord's riches cannot become their riches, and they have nothing to give to others. Therefore, whether or not we are useful in God's hand depends on whether the Holy Spirit has done a work in us. A Christian must not be so fallen as to have no intervention from the Holy Spirit, as if he is destined to poverty. We believe that the Lord does not let go of anyone who commits himself into His hands. We believe that every trial is for enlarging and enriching us. Once a man passes through a trial, he becomes that much richer. Every time a man faces a distress, he knows God that much more. In this way, he becomes gradually qualified to supply God's children in the church.

One sister was saved at the age of thirteen and lived until she was a hundred and three. When she was a hundred years old, a brother went to her and asked why God had kept her on earth for so long. She answered quietly, "God leaves me here to pray and pray." She was indeed a rich person! Another sister was bedridden for forty years, of which thirty-five years she could not hear anything. When a brother went to see her, she said, "I was once very active, running busily here and there. But I neglected the crucial work of prayer in the church. I have been lying here for forty years and every day I fulfill the work of prayer." She did not become angry, impatient, or murmur. On the contrary, she accomplished wonderful works. Her distress had enlarged and enriched her, and her riches had become the riches of the church.

Some brothers and sisters are not that eloquent in the church; they are not that knowledgeable, yet they can pray. Whenever they hear about something, they pray for it. They pray for the sick and pray for the saints who are in trouble. They continue to supply the church through their prayers. Some brothers and sisters only meet; they never pray. Or they only listen to messages; they never pray. These ones have nothing to give to the church. They have not passed through the discipline of the Spirit and do not know what spiritual reality is. They are poor. Some brothers and sisters, in the eyes of man, ought to have been crushed. Yet they are still not crushed because some others have been supplying them. Hence, the riches of life are not a matter of words of doctrine, but a matter of going through something before the Lord to the extent that one renders the supply to the church.

Day by day, the Spirit is seeking the opportunity to lead us into spiritual reality. If we do not accept the discipline of the Holy Spirit, He will not have the opportunity to lead us into spiritual reality. Often when difficulties come, some choose the easy way, and others try to circumvent the proper path. They may bypass the difficulties, but they have lost their opportunity for the Holy Spirit to lead them into spiritual reality. The Spirit will not have the chance to work in them to the extent that their portion becomes the church's. If a person runs away from the discipline of the Holy Spirit, he cannot expect to enter into spiritual reality; instead, he will lose his chance of being enlarged and enriched.

Brothers and sisters, we must accept the discipline of the Holy Spirit before we can be enlarged and before we can supply the church. We need a more complete and thorough consecration so that the Lord's Spirit can have the opportunity to do His work in us and lead us into spiritual reality. May we learn something more day by day before the Lord, and may we have more deposit day by day, so that what we have learned and deposited within will become the riches of the church. These riches will one day be manifested in the new heaven and new earth. Brothers and sisters, no gold or precious stone can escape the fire, and no pearl can come about without some pain. Let us pray that the Lord would deliver us from vain talk and all kinds of poverty, and let us ask Him to show us more and more what spiritual reality is. May the Lord lead us through His Spirit into all spiritual reality.

OBSESSION AND GOD'S LIGHT

Scripture Reading: Isa. 50:10-11; Psa. 36:9

Spiritual reality is that which is true. It is the truth that sets us free. However, a Christian often does not touch that which is true; instead, he falls into falsehood, and he is deceived and bound by the deception. He does not see the true nature of matters, but is deceived to think that he is very clear. What he thinks and does is totally wrong, and yet he thinks that he is very right. This kind of condition is known as "obsession." Those who are obsessed need God's light before they can be delivered from their obsession. Let us first consider what obsession is.

WHAT IS OBSESSION?

Obsession is self-deception. An obsessed person is like the person described in 1 John 1:8. An obsessed person deceives himself. If a man knows that he has sinned, yet tells others that he has not sinned, this is a lie. But if a man has sinned, yet believes that he has not sinned, this is self-deception. Lying is knowing that one has sinned but telling others that he has not sinned. Being obsessed is having clearly sinned yet, at the same time, thinking that one is as wonderful and as sinless as the Lord Jesus, even to the point that he believes and says that he has no sin. Lying is knowing that one has sinned and trying to deceive others. Being obsessed is believing that one has no sin and telling others that he has no sin, when he has really sinned. In other words, lying is deceiving others, while being obsessed is deceiving oneself. The content of lying and obsession are the same; there is sin in both cases. But in one case, a man's conscience knows that he has sinned, yet he deceives others by saying that he has not sinned. In the other case, a man's mind tells him that he has not sinned, and in his heart he also believes that he has not sinned. Those who deceive others are lying, while those who deceive themselves are obsessed. All obsessed persons are self-deceiving persons. All obsessed persons spend so much time considering themselves that they fall into obsession. Many proud people have become obsessed because they not only try to make others believe that they are a certain kind of person, but they themselves believe that they are that kind of person!

Paul was once obsessed. When Stephen was being stoned to death, Paul "approved of his killing" (Acts 8:1). He was obsessed within. When he wrote to the church in Philippi, he mentioned his former condition: "As to zeal, persecuting the church" (Phil. 3:6). He thought that he had to persecute the church in order to serve God with zeal. When men suffered harm, his heart rejoiced. But, according to his consideration, this was not enough. He "went to the high priest and asked for letters from him to Damascus for the synagogues, so that if he found any who were of the Way, both men and women, he might bring them bound to Jerusalem" (Acts 9:1-2). He believed that by doing this, he was serving God with zeal. But was this right? His desire to serve God was right. But it was wrong for him to persecute the church and think that by doing so, he was serving God. He was wrong, yet he believed that he was right. This is obsession.

In John 16:2 the Lord Jesus describes some people who are obsessed. He says, "They will put you out of the synagogues; but an hour is coming for every one who kills you to think that he is offering service to God." To think that one is serving God by killing the Lord's disciples is to fall into obsession.

Obsession is a matter of the heart. It is doing the wrong thing yet saying in the heart that it is right. If a man does something wrong, yet stubbornly says with his mouth that it is right, this is lying. But if a man does something wrong, and not only says with his mouth but even believes in his heart that it is right, this is obsession. Lying is being stubborn outside and being shriveled inside. In this case, the more confident one is outwardly, the more timid he is inwardly. But obsession is being stubborn both outwardly and inwardly. It is being confident both outwardly and inwardly to the extent that even the conscience seems to justify the act.

The symptom of obsession is thinking and believing that a wrong thing is right to the point that one cannot say that it is wrong. This is being obsessed. There are those who imagine that something is happening with others when nothing actually is happening. The imagination goes so far that they become convinced of a certain matter, and they even come up with proofs and evidences to support their imagination. This also is obsession. Some Christians want to do something or desire to achieve certain goals. In the beginning they have some feeling that what they want to do may not be right. But later, as their thoughts are set in that direction, the more they think about it, the more they feel that it is right, and the more real and true the things become. In the end, they believe that it is absolutely right. They consider it to be the truth, and they tell others that it is the truth. This also is obsession. One can be so obsessed that when others use God's Word and prove to him that he is wrong, he will still not take heed. It is not easy to help or correct an obsessed Christian, because he believes that his conscience says he is right.

We must be very careful not to have any intention of deceiving others. Even when we say something inaccurate by accident, we should correct it. If we try to consciously say an inaccurate word, we will first deceive others, but in the end, we will fall into self-deception.

There was a brother who wanted to be zealous for the Lord. He felt that he would not appear zealous enough if he prayed with his natural voice. As a result, he tried to generate a different sound. When he prayed this way in the beginning, he felt somewhat strange, and he was conscious that it was not his own voice. But after a long time, he forgot what his original voice was like. Others could feel the unnatural tone in his prayer, yet he thought that it was very natural indeed. Regarding something unnatural as natural is to be obsessed. In the beginning when he was pretending, there was still the feeling, but after he became obsessed, the feeling was gone; he thought that what he had was real. This shows us the pitiful condition of a man who is obsessed.

Examples of Obsession in Malachi

In the Old Testament, there is one book which shows us what obsessed people are like. This book is Malachi. In 1:2 it says, "I have loved you, says Jehovah." This is a fact. Yet the Israelites said, "How have You loved us?" This is obsession. The word which came out of the mouth of the Israelites was different from ordinary lying. They were not afraid to say to God, "How have You loved us?" This proves that they sincerely believed in their heart that God had not loved them. They did not believe the facts, they took falsehood as truth. This is being obsessed.

Malachi 1:6 says, "A son honors his father, and a servant his lord. Therefore if I am a Father, where is My honor? And if I am the Lord, where is My fear? says Jehovah of hosts to you, O priests who despise My name." This is God's word. Yet they said, "How have we despised Your name?" They did not fear Jehovah, yet they believed that they had not despised His name. This is obsession.

Verse 7 says, "You offer defiled bread upon My altar." This is God's word. Yet they said, "How have we defiled You?" They were wrong, yet they believed that they were right. This is obsession.

Malachi 2:13 says, "And this second thing you do: You cover the altar of Jehovah with tears, with weeping and sighing, so that He no longer regards the sacrifice or receives it with pleasure from your hand." These are facts. Yet they said, "For what reason?" (v. 14). They did something wrong, yet they did not believe that there was such a thing. This is obsession.

Verse 17 says, "You have wearied Jehovah with your words." This is a fact. Yet they said, "How have we wearied Him?" They wearied God, yet they did not believe that they had done so. This is obsession.

Malachi 3:7 says, "From the days of your fathers you have turned aside from My statutes and have not kept them. Return to Me, and I will return to you, says Jehovah of hosts." This is God's word. Yet they asked God, "How shall we return?" It seems as if they had never gone away from God's ordinances. They believed that they did not need to turn any further. This is obsession.

Verse 8 says, "Will a man rob God? Yet you have robbed Me." This is God's word. Yet they said, "How have we robbed You?" They robbed God, yet they believed that they had not done anything. This is obsession.

Verse 13 says, "Your words have been strongly against Me, says Jehovah." This is a fact. Yet they said, "What have we spoken against You?" Their words had been strong against God, yet they believed that they had not done anything. This is obsession.

Examples of Obsession in the Gospel of John

The New Testament also has a book which speaks a great deal about obsession. It is the Gospel of John. The following are some examples.

John 5:43 says, "I have come in the name of My Father, and you do not receive Me; if another comes in his own name, you will receive him." The Israelites seemed to be perfectly at peace with their conscience when they rejected the Lord Jesus. This is obsession.

Verse 44 says, "How can you believe when you receive glory from one another and do not seek the glory that is from the only God?" They did not seek the real glory; they sought that which is not glory. What is this? This is obsession.

John 7:19 says, "Has not Moses given you the law? Yet none of you keeps the law. Why do you seek to kill Me?" This is the Lord's word. The crowd answered, "You have a demon! Who is seeking to kill You?" (v. 20). They were obsessed by their lies. Otherwise, they would not have said, "You have a demon." They wanted to kill the Lord, yet they were so obsessed that they thought the Lord had a demon.

Verse 27 says, "But we know where this man is from; yet when the Christ comes, no one knows where He is from." This is again lying to the point of obsession.

THE SYMPTOMS OF OBSESSION

It is a pitiful and tragic thing to be obsessed. Those who

are obsessed are in a very abnormal condition. Let us consider a few examples of obsession.

Some Christians are obsessed in their speaking. On the one hand, they say something yet believe that they have never said it. On the other hand, they may not say something yet believe that they have said it. Others may not have said something, yet they think that others have said something, and they are convinced that such a thing has been said. Such Christians are not only lying; they are obsessed. Lying is speaking something false while being conscious of it. Being obsessed is speaking something false without being conscious of it. Lying is speaking something false and then realizing that it is wrong. Being obsessed is speaking something false and then thinking that one is right. Some Christians are so obsessed that they take lies for truths, wrongs for right, and falsehoods for facts.

At the beginning, these Christians lie to deceive others. But in the end, they deceive themselves. When one lies, he first deceives one brother, five brothers, and then ten brothers. All the brothers suffer. Yet in the end he pays a great price because this darkness leads him into obsession. He becomes habitual in his lying, and he lies to such an extent that he becomes convinced that he is speaking the truth. He becomes obsessed. In the beginning, lying deceives others. But in the end, it brings one into obsession. For a person to tell another that such and such a thing happened and how real it was, when nothing actually happened, is to lie. But a while later, the same person may go and tell another the same thing, and two people can be deceived. He may then go and tell two more the same thing in detail, and two more people are deceived. When he first lied, he might have felt a little uneasiness, and he might have realized that a Christian should not do such a thing. But as time goes on, he begins to lose his feeling, and he becomes more and more convinced in himself, believing that what he says is true. This is obsession. Being obsessed is fabricating something to deceive others to the extent that eventually one believes it himself.

Some Christians are obsessed with the matter of giving testimonies. A brother once heard many testimonies from others about answers to prayers, God's blessings to works, and God's deliverance in troubles. These testimonies stirred up a kind of fantasy within him, and he began to think that his prayers also were answered. He believed that God's blessings were in his works and that he had experienced God's deliverance in troubles. Actually, none of these were facts; they were all his imaginations. But whenever he had the opportunity, he would rise up to give his testimonies, and he described them with such detail that they appeared to be very real. In his mouth something ordinary would become an extraordinary event, and something not so wonderful would become something quite wonderful. After he testified this way again and again, he began to believe what he said. At a certain point, he could no longer tell what part was genuine and what part was fabricated. When a man falls so deeply into self-deception, he begins to believe in himself that everything is true. This is obsession.

Some Christians are obsessed with sickness. They do not have any illness, but they think that they are sick with this and that kind of disease. Many such illnesses come from self-love. They are not really sick, and their sicknesses are not recognized by medical doctors. But they love and protect themselves too much. If they have a slight discomfort, they say that they are sick of this or that. When their heart beats a little faster, they say that they have heart disease. When they cough a little, they say that they have tuberculosis of the lungs. If a doctor truthfully tells them that they are not sick, they say that the doctor is not a good doctor. If the doctor agrees with them and says that they are sick, they say that the doctor is good. They say that they are sick, when in fact they are healthy. This is self-love to the point of obsession. In the beginning, they say that they are sick in order to gain the sympathy of their relatives, friends, and family members. But in the end, they truly believe that they are sick. Their heart has created the sickness out of nothing. This is obsession. Being obsessed is deceiving oneself with something fabricated to the extent that one does not realize that he has been deceived by himself.

Some Christians are obsessed with fear. They fear in their

heart, but there is no actual cause for fear. They might have been apprehensive at the beginning about certain things. But in the end, they become genuinely afraid of these things. Even if you give them all kinds of reasons to not be afraid, they still cannot believe you. If anyone tells them that they need not fear, they fear all the more. This is being obsessed.

Some Christians are obsessed with speculations. Because of the lack of light, they often take speculation as fact. First they speculate that certain people would do certain things, go to certain places, and say certain words. Later, they believe that the person has indeed done these things, been to those places, and said those words. They can become so obsessed that they consider that something is there when it is actually not there. It may clearly be a case of wrongly blaming a person, but they believe that they have the facts. This is obsession. It is obsession to think that a person is a certain way when he really is not, or to believe that a certain person has done certain things when he really has not. Being obsessed is taking speculations as reality.

There is another kind of obsession. Some Christians are very seeking and are very desirous of going on in a proper way before the Lord. Yet they do not have any light. Something may not be wrong, yet they think that they have done wrong, and they constantly worry about it to the extent that they say the Lord will no longer forgive them and the blood will no longer cleanse them. In God's eyes, they have not sinned. Yet they are very certain that they have sinned. They think that they have done an irreparable wrong and committed an unforgivable sin. They are full of sorrow, and they weep. Thinking that one confession is not enough, they confess ten times or even a hundred times. Even while they are confessing continuously, they feel that their sin is still present. What is this? This is obsession. One can be obsessed with more than just bad things. It is even possible to be obsessed with the sense of sin. If a seeking Christian does not have the light, he will condemn what he has not committed. This is obsession. Being obsessed is believing that something is real when in fact it is not.

Isaiah 5:20 says, "Woe to those who call good evil, / And

evil good; / Who make darkness light, / And light darkness; / Who make bitterness sweetness, / And sweetness bitterness!" A man can be so obsessed that he calls good evil, and evil good; makes darkness light, and light darkness; makes bitterness sweetness, and sweetness bitterness. He can be obviously wrong and yet be still very confident that he is right. This is very pitiful. The worst thing that can happen to a Christian is to have sinned and be ignorant of it. To have sinned is a matter of defilement, but to be ignorant of sin is a matter of darkness. Defilement is dangerous enough, but if it is complemented with darkness, the danger is even greater. If a Christian lives in darkness, it will not be easy for him to go on, because he does not see.

There are many different symptoms of obsession. It is possible for a Christian to be obsessed with his own thoughts, others' thoughts, his own words, others' words, his own spiritual condition, his own sins, or anything he has. Obsession is also a very common thing, and it can happen to any Christian. Of course, some are obsessed to a smaller degree, others are obsessed to a greater degree, while some are obsessed to a very serious degree. Therefore, we must pay attention to this matter.

THE REASONS FOR OBSESSION

There are always reasons for Christians to be obsessed. We must now find a few basic reasons for obsession from the Bible.

Love of Darkness

One great reason for obsession is the fact that men love darkness and do not love light. When a man does not prefer light but prefers darkness, there is bias in his heart, and it becomes easy for him to be obsessed. A man may try at first to avoid difficulties, troubles, and the light by saying that he is right. But in the end, he begins to believe that he is right and good, and he becomes obsessed. The Israelites rejected the Lord Jesus because they loved the darkness rather than the light (John 3:19). They did not have the light, and they dwelt in darkness. Therefore, they considered it justified to reject and hate the Lord Jesus. The Lord said, "If I did not do among them the works which no one else has done, they would not have sin; but now they have both seen and hated both Me and My Father" (15:24). This is because they were obsessed. They hated the Lord Jesus without cause (v. 25). We must realize that wherever there is darkness and wherever there is a lack of light, there is a wrong view, wrong confidence, wrong self-trust, and wrong judgment. Everything that is wrong has the element of obsession in it. The result of not loving the light is obsession.

Pride

Pride is another great reason for obsession. Obadiah 3 says, "The arrogance of your heart has beguiled you." This shows us that another reason for self-deception is pride. Those who are self-deceived to the point of obsession are probably proud ones. A Christian may start out with the intention of gaining vainglory and position before men, and then may begin to pretend and deceive others. Gradually, he begins to deceive himself, and he becomes obsessed in the end. Once a Christian becomes proud, it is easy for him to fantasize that he has something, that he possesses something, and gradually he will regard his fantasy as reality; the result is obsession. Brothers and sisters, do not think that pride is a small sin. Pride can easily lead to obsession. This is why we have to learn to be humble.

Not Receiving the Love of the Truth

Another great reason for obsession is not receiving the love of the truth. Second Thessalonians 2:10-11 tells us that God sends to those who "did not receive the love of the truth...an operation of error that they might believe the lie." This is a terrible end. When a man believes in lies, the result is obsession. To believe in lies is to believe that there is something when there is actually nothing. When a man does not receive the love of the truth, surely he believes in lies, and when he believes in lies, he is obsessed.

Proverbs 23:23 says, "Buy the truth, and sell it not; / also wisdom, and instruction, and understanding." Truth is something that we have to buy, something that requires a price. We would be blessed if our hearts were ready to love and receive only God's truth at any price. But men often do not have a heart to receive the love of the truth. On the contrary, they twist the truth and annul the truth; they hope that this and that are not the truth. They end up believing that this and that are not the truth. They make the truth untruth and the untruth truth, and they appear to be very confident about it. This is being obsessed. We must realize that if a man does not receive the love of the truth once, it will be difficult for him to see the truth later.

A brother who studied in a seminary once went to a theological professor to ask about the matter of baptism. The brother said, "I saw before the Lord that I have been crucified with Christ, that I have died, and that I should be buried. Therefore, I ought to be baptized. What would you say?" The professor said, "I had a similar experience when I was in the seminary. I was about to graduate, and I saw that I was dead and that I ought to be buried and baptized. But if I had been baptized, I would no longer have been able to work in my denomination. I prayed and felt that I would wait until I graduated and was a pastor. Many years have passed since I graduated and became a pastor. I am still not baptized, and everything still seems okay. You should concentrate on your study. After you graduate, you will be a pastor and such questions will not bother you anymore." Disobeying the truth and thinking that one can live in peace is obsession. Fortunately, the brother did not follow the professor's advice. Brothers and sisters, when our hearts are not absolute, it will be easy for us to be obsessed.

Not Seeking the Glory That Is from the Only God

Another reason for obsession is not seeking the glory that is from the only God. The Lord Jesus said, "How can you believe when you receive glory from one another and do not seek the glory that is from the only God?" (John 5:44). This shows us that the Israelites rejected the Lord and lost eternal life by seeking for another kind of glory. How pitiful this is! The Israelites' lust for glory turned their hearts towards lies.

As a result they believed the lies, began to think highly of themselves, and were obsessed.

SEEING LIGHT IN GOD'S LIGHT

Obsession is a tragic thing. God's children must not be obsessed. Those who are obsessed do not see the true nature of things. In the following paragraphs we will consider the way to see the true nature of things and the way to be saved from obsession.

Isaiah 50:10-11 says, "Who among you fears Jehovah; / Who hears the voice of His servant; / Who walks in darkness / And has no light? / Let him trust in the name of Jehovah, / And rely on his God. / Behold, all of you who kindle a fire, / Who surround yourselves with firebrands, / Walk into the light of your fire / And into the firebrands which you have lit. / You will have this from My hand: / You will lie down in torment."

Verse 10 is not that easy to understand. If we change the punctuation according to the following way, the meaning may become somewhat clearer: "Who among you fears Jehovah; who hears the voice of His servant—who walks in darkness and has no light? Let him trust in the name of Jehovah, and rely on his God." This means, "Is there anyone among you who fears the Lord and obeys the voice of His servant?" If someone wants to obey the voice of the Lord's servant yet walks in darkness and does not have the light, what should he do? He should "trust in the name of Jehovah, / And rely on his God."

Verse 11 says, "Behold, all of you who kindle a fire, / Who surround yourselves with firebrands, / Walk into the light of your fire / And into the firebrands which you have lit. / You will have this from My hand: / You will lie down in torment." When the Israelites were walking in darkness and did not have the light, it was natural for them to kindle a fire and surround themselves with firebrands. Is it not good that they walked in the light of their fire and in the firebrands that they kindled? No, the result was that they would lie down in torment. Spiritual darkness cannot be removed by human fires. Light comes from God alone and does not come from man. Man's fire will never bring about genuine spiritual sight.

Our own fire can never be the source of spiritual light. Some Christians have said, "How can you say that I was wrong? I do not think that I was at all wrong. I do not feel that I was wrong at all." You may think that you are not wrong, you may feel that you are not wrong, and you may believe that you are not wrong, but are you reliable? Some Christians have said, "I have considered a certain matter for a long time. I can say for sure that it should be done this way or that way." Can you make judgment just because you have thought a matter over? According to God's Word, this is not the way for Christians to know things. You can try your best to think, but what you come up with is just human fire. A Christian cannot go on in the spiritual pathway by his own fire. He should trust in the name of the Lord and rely upon his God. Only then will he see and only then will he be able to go on in the spiritual pathway. Many times, the more we think by ourselves, the more confused and deceived we become. We must see that spiritual light does not come from our feelings or our thoughts. The more a person searches inwardly for light, the more he will not find light, because light is not there.

Let us read Psalm 36:9: "For with You is the fountain of life; / In Your light we see light." This shows us that through God's light, a man sees light and the true condition of things. "In Your light we see light." The first light is the enlightening light, and the second light denotes the true nature of things. This means that we can only see the true nature of anything when we are in the light of God. One only sees the true nature of something when he lives in God's light.

Brothers and sisters, it makes a great difference where we live. We must live in God's light before we can be one who sees. Some Christians command our respect not because they are good men, but because they live before the Lord. First John 1:5 says, "God is light." All those who know God know the light. We can find God from those who know the light. Once we meet a person who knows God's light, he will know our true condition, and he will be able to point out our error. He is not fastidious; he is merely sharp with his inward eyes, and he can discover the true condition of things easily. Those who do not have the light may consider some things very good. But those who have the light will discern the true nature of these things. Only those who live in God's light will see light. Only those who live in God's light will see the true nature of things. When a man is under the strong light of the sun, there is no need for him to use a torchlight. Those who are under God's light have no need of human fire. If a man lives in God's light, the true nature of things will be as clear and bright as light itself. If a man is under God's light, he will discern the intrinsic nature of things. The only time a person genuinely knows himself is when he knows himself under God's light. If we are not in God's light, we may sin, but we will not feel the evil of sin. We may fail, but we will not feel the shame of failure. We may perform well outwardly, but inwardly we will not know how deceitful we are. We may be humble outwardly, but inwardly we will not know how proud we are. We may appear gentle outwardly, but inwardly we will not know how stubborn we are. We may appear spiritual outwardly, but inwardly we will not know how fleshly we are. When God's light shines on us, our true condition will be exposed, and we will see and admit how blind we have been!

The difference between the Old Testament and the New Testament is that the Old Testament shows men what is right and what is wrong through outward laws, while the New Testament shows men the true nature of things through the Holy Spirit dwelling within. We often see our error through doctrines, but we do not see our error through God's light. We have to realize that it is superficial to see our error through doctrines. Only when we see our error through God's light is there a thorough seeing. When we are in God's light we see what God sees. This is seeing the light in the light.

In order to not be obsessed, we need to live in God's light. But the greatest temptation for us is to light our own fire. Whenever we encounter problems, we try to search inwardly to find out what is right and what is wrong. Brothers and sisters, this is not the way God wants us to take. We have to humble ourselves and admit that we are not trustworthy, that our judgments are not trustworthy, and that our thoughts and conduct are not trustworthy. It is possible for us to make

mistakes. What we consider as right may not be right, and
what we consider as wrong may not be wrong. What we consider as sweet may not be sweet, and what we consider as
bitter may not be bitter. What we consider as light may not be
light, and what we consider as darkness may not be darkness.
We should not replace God's light with our own light; we
should receive our light from God.

The Lord said, "The lamp of the body is the eye. If therefore your eye is single, your whole body will be full of light;
but if your eye is evil, your whole body will be dark. If then
the light that is in you is darkness, how great is the darkness!" (Matt. 6:22-23). Once a Christian loses the inward
light, he will become obsessed. It is very pitiful to fail to see
what we should see and fail to know what we should know.
We must ask God to enlighten us so that we can touch Him.
The Christian life should not be one that is filled with questions, doubts, or uncertainties. We should see if something is
right or not right. If we see, we will not be obsessed.

The Lord said, "If anyone resolves to do His will, he will
know concerning the teaching, whether it is of God or whether
I speak from Myself" (John 7:17). The condition for receiving
the light is seeking after God's will. Whenever we are faced
with any situation, we should not be so confident to say
whether it is right or wrong. We need to ask God for His
mercy, so that we may have an absolute desire to do His will.
Stubbornness, selfishness, and self-justification can all shut
out God's light. If we want God's light, we need to be gentle
and not selfish or self-assured. We must be humble. May the
Lord save us day by day to live in His light, so that we know
what is real and what is true. May the Lord deliver us from
lies and obsessions.

OTHER BOOKS
Living Strec

W0006504

Available at
Christian bookstores, or contact Living Stream Ministry
2431 W. La Palma Ave. • Anaheim, CA 92801
1-800-549-5164 • www.livingstream.com